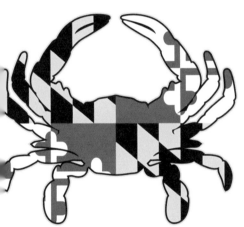

My Maryland Book
A-Z

Elizabeth Ann

Archway Publishing books may be ordered through booksellers or by contacting:

Archway Publishing
1663 Liberty Drive
Bloomington, IN 47403
www.archwaypublishing.com
844-669-3957

ISBN: 978-1-6657-2832-4 (sc)
ISBN: 978-1-6657-2833-1 (e)

Print information available on the last page.

Archway Publishing rev. date: 08/09/2022

This book is dedicated to my Son, Tyler, my Daughter, Danielle, and to Michael, the man who reminds me never to give up on your dreams.

MARYLAND
A-Z

A   -   Aquarium
B   -   Bay Bridge
C   -   Crabs
D   -   Dairy Farmers - Ice Cream
E   -   Ellicott City
F   -   Fishing
G   -   Geese
H   -   Horse Country
I   -   Inner Harbor
J   -   Jelly Fish
K   -   Kites
L   -   Light Houses
M   -   Museums
N   -   Naval Academy
O   -   Ocean City
P   -   Port Discovery Children's Museum
Q   -   Quarry
R   -   Ravens Football
S   -   State Fair
T   -   Trails
U   -   Umbrellas
V   -   Vineyards
W   -   Waterways
X   -   Xmas Tree
Y   -   Yachts
Z   -   Zoo

Off to the **A**quarium (uh-kweh-ree-uhm) for an adventure for the day. You will be amazed watching the sharks swim while walking up and down the ramp. The aquarium is located in downtown Baltimore City.

How exciting to drive over the **B**ay **B**ridge, (ba-brij). Look out your window to view the Chesapeake Bay. What do you see?

Maryland **C**rab, (krab), also known as a crustacean. They have five pair of legs, the first pair of which are considered pinchers, which will grab you if you get too close. They are a favorite for most once they are steamed and flavored with seasoning. Did you know there are different names for the crabs? They are called females, males, peelers, which will turn into a soft-shell crab, then turn back into a hard crab.

Dairy (dere) Farmers in Maryland produce cheese and ice cream. So many places to visit in our wonderful state to enjoy a big scoop of ice cream. What is your favorite flavor?

Ellicott (el-i-kuht) City is a quaint little town in Howard County, Maryland. This town stays strong. Whether you are shopping, eating, or strolling along the sidewalks, downtown Ellicott City won't disappoint.

Fish in Maryland. Whether you are fishing on the Chesapeake Bay, a local lake, or a pond, it is a fun day for many. In case you are wondering, a lake is deeper than a pond.

A few of the fish you can find in Maryland are: Striped bass, Bluegills, Catfish, Drum, Flounder, Perch, Trout, and Shark.

The Striped Bass, also known as the Rockfish, is the State Fish.

Have you ever heard an unusual sound above you and looked up to see a **G**oose (goos) flying close by? Did you see more than one?

Canadian Geese are common in Maryland. Most geese like lakes and ponds and you will see them hanging out in fields too.

Driving around Baltimore County, you are sure to see a **H**orse (hors). They are strong and beautiful.

We can't forget about the incredible Assateague Horses. They live at the park and they are wild. They survive the many climate changes in Maryland, from the heat of the summer to the cold of our winter.

The Inner (in-er) Harbor (hahr-ber) is located in Baltimore, Maryland, on the water. At the Inner Harbor, you can visit the Maryland Science Center and the National Aquarium. There are shops and restaurants to visit too.

Jellyfish (jel-ee fish) also are called nettles. A Jellyfish has a transparent body and looks like there is an umbrella on top. The creatures are found in the Chesapeake Bay where the water is the saltiest. Be careful when you see one, because they sting.

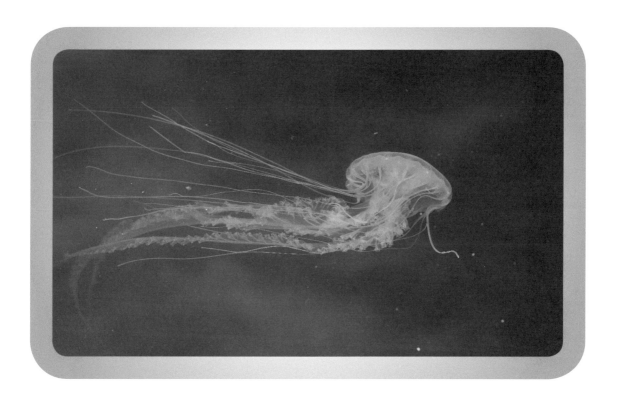

Have you ever been at the beach or an open field flying a **K**ite (kīt), or just watching one whip through the sky? They come in all shapes and sizes. The air pushes them up on a windy day.

Light (līt) **H**ouse (hous). They were built to guide sailors to safety long ago. You can find a light house near or in the water. They are different in sizes and colors, but you will know when you see one.

Museums (myoo-zee-uhms) in Maryland are places to learn. So much to see, whether it is paintings or artifacts. Going to a museum will fill your mind. Walk in and open your eyes to see all of the wonders that museums offer.

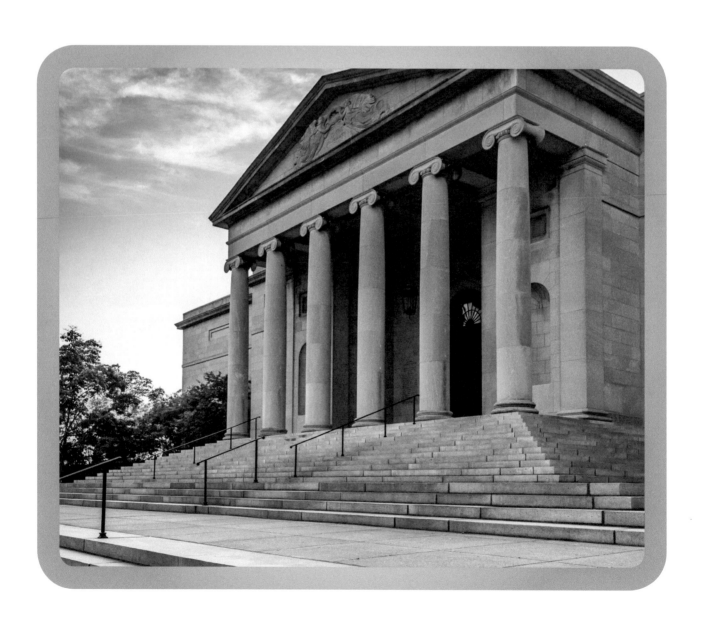

The United States **N**aval (navēl) Academy (ə kadəmē) is located in Annapolis, Maryland. The Naval Academy prepares their recruits to become professional officers in the Navy and Marines.

Visiting Ocean (ōSHən) City (sidē), Maryland takes you on a journey. From splashing in the water while the waves crash down on your feet, to wiggling your toes in the warm sand, to having fun playing putt-putt golf or on the water slides. There are many places to eat – from diners and pubs to restaurants that will fill your stomach with delicious food.

Port Discovery Children's Museum is located in Baltimore City, Maryland. It is a great place for children to play and learn. Three floors filled with activities that will fill your mind, whether you are being creative, thinking, or having lots of fun getting exercise.

Quarry. (kwôrē). This is a place that usually has a large hole in the ground, sometimes called a pit. Stone and other materials are extracted to build homes or other places where marble and other hard stones are used.

Ravens (rā vən's) Football (fút ból). Do you wear purple on Friday during Football Season? Or a Ravens shirt to support the football team? In Maryland, many, young and old, enjoy wearing purple, because they love football.

State Fair. When fall approaches in Maryland, we know it is time to make our way to Timonium, where the Maryland State Fair is held. You will see food trucks, horse racing, farm animals, and rides to enjoy. What a fun time for all.

Trails (trāls) in Maryland can be a short walk or miles, even ending up in a different state. Whatever distance you can travel, there is a trail for most. Lots of trails are located in the woods, and most have paths that allows you a smooth walk. Nature at its best, whether you are on the C&O Canal Trail (Chesapeake and Ohio Canal Trail) or the NCR Trail (Northern Central Railroad Trail). Two of my favorite places to walk or take a bike ride.

C&O Canal Trail

NCR Trail

Umbrella. (uhm-brel-uh) If you love being outside when it is hot, I am sure you have seen umbrellas line the beach. They protect you from the sun. Whether you rent one at the beach or bring your own, it will help you from getting sun burned.

Vineyard. (vin-yerd). Open fields, sun, and rich soil produce grapes. These grapes allow wine to be made in my State. In recent years, wineries have opened their doors and allowed families to visit and enjoy the day at the vineyard. The vineyards offer more than wine to families. My favorite vineyard is called, Boordy which is located in Hydes, Maryland.

Waterways (waw-ter-weys) in Maryland can be found throughout the State. Maryland has 23 counties and one city. My favorite waterways are the Potomac River and the Chesapeake Bay. Whether riding my bike along the Potomac or fishing with my Dad on the Chesapeake Bay, you will always see a smile on my face. Did you know that the Potomac runs into the Chesapeake Bay?

Xmas Tree. Also known as the Christmas tree. Normally an evergreen that is decorated in the spirit and celebration of Christmas. What is your favorite? The Douglas Fir or a Blue Spruce? Whether your tree is real or artificial, you can decorate your tree anyway that you like.

Yachts (yats) in Maryland. If you drive up to a Marina, you are sure to see these large boats floating in the water. To be considered a Yacht, the vessel must be at least 33 feet long.

The Maryland **Z**oo. This is where you can see animals from around the world. It is an experience that you will never forget. Whether you are watching the strong lions roam around, adorable penguins waddling around in the water, or the monkeys swinging on the limbs.

The End

I hope you enjoyed "My Maryland Book".

Printed in the United States
by Baker & Taylor Publisher Services